BBC MUSIC GU

BERLIOZ ORCHESTRAL MUSIC

BBC MUSIC GUIDES

Berlioz Orchestral Music

HUGH MACDONALD

UNIVERSITY OF WASHINGTON PRESS
SEATTLE

First published 1969 by the British Broadcasting Corporation

University of Washington Press edition first published 1969
Library of Congress Catalog Card Number 73-80516
Printed in England

Works discussed

Berlioz and the Orchestra

In his *Treatise on Modern Instrumentation and Orchestration*, published in 1843, Berlioz concludes his discussion of the individual instruments with a section entitled 'The Orchestra' as though it, too, were an instrument in its own right. Indeed this is precisely his justification for setting out the ways in which an orchestra should properly be constituted, placed, and directed. A violinist will teach the correct way to hold a fiddle; Berlioz had some instructive words on the correct way to manage and write for an orchestra.

He was drawn to the orchestra as his chosen medium by instinct, and it was probably fortunate that he never mastered any instrument, not even the ubiquitous piano. He learned orchestral technique by the study of the masters – Gluck, Weber, Spontini, Beethoven, and the rest – and by finding out the exact capabilities and timbres of individual instruments, and it was on this raw material that his imagination worked to produce countless new sonorities, very striking when considered as a totality, crucially instructive for later composers, and nearly all exactly tailored to their dramatic or expressive purpose. Berlioz did not see himself as a master chef serving up orchestral titbits in ever more exciting dressings, but as a serious performer upon the most elaborate and powerful of instruments, the orchestra itself.

It was as a player of the orchestra that Berlioz sought to advertise his claims as a composer. For thirty years from the mid-1820s – intensively at first, less so as time went on – he belaboured Paris audiences with concerts for which he composed the music, hired the hall, engaged and (later) conducted the musicians, and bore the financial losses; he was even expected to supply the string players with mutes and spare strings. Rarely would established organisations play his music and rarely would established orchestras engage him to conduct them. This harassing concert life was the life he would willingly have given himself to more fully if it had been at all self-supporting and if it had enabled him to give up his detested career as a music critic. (Ironically this was a profession he also excelled at, but it helped him little as a composer.) Every time he gave a concert he had a different orchestra, and his attempts to found a regular Philharmonic Society in rivalry to the established Société des Concerts quickly failed. The general view of the musical establishment was that giving orchestral concerts was Berlioz's way of covering up his deficiency on any other instrument, and his *Memoirs* tell us of comic but distressing incidents when stage-door keepers and the like would refuse to admit him to concert halls without the ordinary evidence that he would be performing there: an instrument under his arm. It must be remembered that baton conductors were still a new phenomenon and that even they were normally drawn from the orchestra's principal string desks.

A comparison is frequently drawn with Paganini on the violin and Liszt on the piano, both of whom exercised a decisive influence upon Berlioz as men and as musicians. What struck him most about these transcendental performers was not so much the dazzling virtuosity of their techniques but their revelation of new and untried resources of their instruments. Berlioz rarely uses the orchestra simply to thrill the nerves; when he does it is extraordinarily exciting, as in the *Hungarian March* or the *Roman Carnival* overture. But he is more intent on widening the orchestral palette and giving it greater flexibility and suggestive resource. He was constantly delighted to find new instruments and new ways of playing the old ones. He befriended the inventor Adolphe Sax and welcomed the many Sax instruments, some into his own scores. He tried muting the woodwind, he explored harmonics on the strings and harp, he extended the range of orchestral percussion, he used trombone pedal notes, he gave the 'extra' woodwind (piccolo, cor anglais, bass clarinet) regular status, he divided the strings into many parts, he used the piano as an orchestral colour. Nothing tried his patience more severely than the instrumentalist who was ignorant of the potential of his instrument or the composer who wrote unimaginatively or tastelessly for the orchestra.

Berlioz's orchestral sound is not difficult to recognise, although it is naturally inseparable from his harmonic and rhythmic style. Certain characteristics recur with obsessive frequency: he usually writes for the woodwind in layers, especially for flute and clarinet in octaves, and woodwind solos are very much rarer in Berlioz than in other composers. The sound of all the woodwind chattering in repeated quavers is very idiosyncratic. He uses four bassoons in preference to two. The horns rarely have the romantic bloom of, say, Weber's music, and are used more as mobile support for either woodwind or fellow brass. Trumpets have the same circumscribed parts as in Beethoven, but Berlioz supplements them at all times with two extra valve trumpets or cornets which are used as a new versatile and brilliant melodic line. Consider the brazen theme in the 'March to the Scaffold' which is unthinkable in Beethoven and totally dependent upon the newly invented valve system. Two orchestral works, the 'Ball' movement of the *Symphonie Fantastique* and the *Francs Juges* overture, have optional obbligato cornet parts for added brilliance.

For Wagner the real source of dynamic power is the horns, but for Berlioz it is the trombones, and it is important to realise that in his day they made a very different sound from the usual trombone tone of today. It was much more wiry and piercing and would contrast very strongly with the horns. Gradually Berlioz came to use the trombones with great subtlety and their use in the last two operas is exemplary in its flexibility. He was as fascinated by the sound of three trombones playing softly in unison as he was by the sinister power of their pedal notes, which are always used to suggest terror or awe. The ophicleide had a much less robust sound than the tuba, although Berlioz welcomed the gradual replacement of the one by the other – which took place during his lifetime. He never writes for the ophicleide as a fourth trombone, but gives it independent duties as a support to the rest of the brass.

The percussion is sometimes greedily and sometimes delicately used, and Berlioz was proud to have rid the section of vulgar associations and given it a new respectability. His writing for strings is probably less distinctive than for wind and could even at times be clumsy; this was not an area that had suffered much neglect by earlier generations. But he cultivated the sound of high violins divided into many parts for ethereal effects, and cellos and basses similarly multi-divided for sombre colours. It is such things as the rushing scales in the bass (see, for example, Ex. 33, p. 60) that really mark Berlioz's individual style.

The section in the *Treatise* on 'The Orchestra' is in fact not concerned with the art of orchestration itself but with the more fundamental matters of numbers, balance, and disposition. Berlioz detested the sound of small theatre orchestras thrown out of balance by imported batteries of bass drums and trombones; he insisted that the strings should be strong enough to match the wind. Another obsession was his care about the placing of instruments in relation to each other. The score of *Romeo and Juliet* has a lengthy preface to explain the exact siting of the various choral and instrumental bodies. In the *Funeral and Triumphal Symphony* the side-drums are explicitly instructed to be a long way from the other percussion. We find the same care over spatial details in the instructions to the three off-stage bands in *The Trojans* and in the insistence that the organ and orchestra of the *Te Deum* should be well separated. The *locus classicus* of grand spatial organisation is the *Requiem*, with its four extra brass bands marked North, South, East, and West. The point of these gigantic forces is not that the effect should be merely loud, but that enormous spaces need enormous sounds to fill them. The sound of huge forces in a huge architectural space has very little in common with noisiness and it is an effect that naturally enough defies capture by any kind of recording technique. Berlioz himself answered all later assaults upon his so-called noisiness:

> Vulgar prejudice considers large orchestras *noisy*; if they are well constituted, well rehearsed, and well conducted, and if they play real music, the correct term is *powerful*. No two expressions are more dissimilar in meaning than these.

Berlioz was not greatly interested in architecture, but St Peter's in Rome and St Paul's in London were two buildings which fired his imagination by their vastness, for he was appalled at the inappropriate piping of eighteen singers and a portable organ in the one and sent into raptures by the immensity of 6,500 children singing in unison in the other. It is the big choral works and *The Trojans* that most clearly reflect his interest in three-dimensional sonority, but the symphonies all betray the same attitude of mind, and the careful directions in every one of his orchestral scores are not to be taken lightly.

Berlioz was interested in orchestral music (with which we must include operatic and choral music with orchestra) to the exclusion of all else. He wrote no piano music and no chamber music, and the best of his songs were sooner or later transcribed for orchestra. This commitment to the most extravagant and unwieldy of musical means is one facet of the idealism which burnt fiercely in many romantic breasts. An unwillingness to compromise mattered almost more than what one actually stood for. Schumann and Liszt both made compromises with their first ideals in a way unthinkable to Berlioz, yet for him it was no idealism for its own sake; he was no *poseur*. Berlioz had a sincere conviction that his proper mode of expression was the orchestra, built upon a private awareness of the power of his imagination and his ability to construct monuments of sound if only circumstances would allow. He pursued this ideal with maniacal resolution, and never allowed his style, his subject-matter, or his media to be dictated or deflected by temptations of an easier progress.

It is a cardinal sin, then, and a mark of deep misunderstanding to condemn *Romeo and Juliet* for being ill-adapted to the concert-giver's needs. The tenor and contralto soloists are barely required, but how can one possibly complain that Berlioz does not use them more in order to justify their presence? His subject had no more room for them. It is *not* absurd for Berlioz to ask for twelve harps at the close of the *Te Deum*'s 'March for the Presentation of the Colours' because that was the effect he wanted. Berlioz was not concerned so much with how many harpists were available (though he would never lose sight of this) as with how many were required to make that exhilarating sound; he would no more accept one or two harps as a maximum than one or two violins. He would not convert *Harold in Italy* into a concerto even for Paganini, because that was not what he set out to write. *The Trojans* was long held to be hopelessly impracticable on the stage, too long and too vast, and this in an age of Wagnerian fervour. The point is that none of these works is impracticable; they simply make unusual demands, and in recent years it has been recurrently shown that if one is prepared to meet these demands in full the idealism and the vision become plain.

When Berlioz descended from his study to the rostrum he became an intensely practical musician yet governed at all times by the spirit of the music. He fought unendingly against the adaptations of classical masters by Fétis, Habeneck, Castil-Blaze, and others; he was the first to put forward the view that is now universal but was then revolutionarily new: that music should be performed according to the taste of the composer and not the taste of the conductor or audience, that it should be enshrined in its own period and not brought up to date. He would not tolerate re-orchestration or 'trombonisation', as he called it. He very rarely compromised with the demands of his own scores, though it was his common practice to replace the two bells in the last movement of the *Fantastic Symphony* by octaves on a grand piano since deep bells were rarely found, then as now. (Modern tubular bells are no nearer to the sound he wanted than a piano.) He would cut whole movements rather than have them played inaccurately or without understanding, and he reckoned that in ninety-nine cases out of a hundred an audience would be insufficiently intelligent and well informed to grasp the later scenes of *Romeo and Juliet*. He withheld publication of his first symphonies for some years in order to prevent inadequate performances.

Berlioz has sometimes been criticised for his self-borrowings, and although we meet with comparatively few cases in the purely orchestral works, it is necessary to explain that they arise most frequently from his determination to give his stronger ideas a better chance. Two ideas were transferred from the *Rob Roy* overture to *Harold in Italy* because they were too good to discard while the overture as a whole was too weak to preserve. I have omitted any discussion of the *Reverie and Caprice* for violin and orchestra in this short study because it was originally a soprano aria in the opera *Benvenuto Cellini* and its translation into instrumental language was not strikingly successful. Other interesting cases of vocal music being transferred to instruments are found at the very opening of the *Fantastic Symphony*, and in the second movement of the *Funeral and Triumphal Symphony*, where the trombone solo declaims a scene for tenor solo from the abandoned opera *Les Francs Juges*.

These adaptations were made possible by Berlioz's refusal to regard the human voice as essentially different from instruments. 'The Voices' also have their appropriate chapter in the *Treatise on Instrumentation*, sandwiched between the Russian bassoon and the timpani. He would see nothing odd in using voices at intervals in a symphony in the same way as he would use, say, the percussion. He even anticipates the twentieth century's use of wordless chorus as a kind of extension of the orchestral medium. This spilling over of vocal into instrumental music has been the cause of much incomprehension amongst those who love to pigeonhole vocal and instrumental forms, and it also makes it difficult to speak of Berlioz's orchestral music as if it were a self-contained body of music. There is constant interpenetration of symphony, cantata, opera, and oratorio, and the enormous choice of forms thrown open to Berlioz by his willingness to let the borderlines blur has thrown musical analysts into confusion. He saw it as the source of great freedom: the forms need no longer dominate the material; the subject-matter could dictate its own forms; it was now possible to construct works like *Lélio*, *Romeo and Juliet*, and *The Damnation of Faust*, having close associations with all kinds of established forms but direct likeness to none. I have excluded discussion of *Lélio* from these pages, since it is not a symphony, and at no point is the orchestra the protagonist. *Romeo and Juliet*, on the other hand, most unquestionably *is* a symphony. The overtures are more clearly defined, some being concert overtures in their own right, others being attached to finished or abortive operas. I have also taken the opportunity to discuss Berlioz's many marches, as they constitute an interesting and important genre in his music.

The Overtures

WAVERLEY

The early overtures divide themselves into pairs, two dating from Berlioz's student years at the Conservatoire, two from the sojourn in Italy. In each case Berlioz was proud of one and neglectful of the other. *Les Francs Juges* was accepted, *Waverley* forgotten; *King Lear* was approved, *Rob Roy* rejected.

The first two, *Les Francs Juges* and *Waverley* were written within a short space of time, and the most likely date is 1827, when Berlioz was 23. In his *Memoirs* Berlioz tells us that *Les Francs Juges* preceded its fellow, and to the end of his life was wont to reflect proudly that it was his first instrumental work. And although *Waverley* is intrinsically a weaker work, it is one of the earliest self-sufficient concert overtures.

Historical considerations apart, *Waverley* is not a startling, nor even fully characteristic work, and after opening Berlioz's momentous first concert on 26 May 1828 it was very rarely taken into his concert repertory. It was published in 1839. On the manuscript Berlioz scribbled a long text made up of sentences from the novel, but later replaced these with the single quotation that now stands at the head of the score:

> Dreams of love and Lady's charms
> Give place to honour and to arms.

We should not look for a specifically Scottish tone, but rather for evocations of the chivalry beloved of the romantic temperament. The simple contrast implicit in the superscription (slow introduction followed by a vigorous *allegro*) appears also in the *Francs Juges* overture and was to serve as a basis for all the others. The later ones extended the pattern by opening with a bold foretaste of the *allegro* before the introduction proper.

Waverley begins with fragmentary ideas of great concentration and audacity. The oboe's solitary note and the heavings of the divided lower strings are essentially new. But before Berlioz has been able to explain to us their significance (they surely probe further than 'Dreams of love') he introduces a melody on the cellos in a placid D major, romance-like and tender and repeated with suggestions of canon in a more elaborate orchestration, already declaring Berlioz's capacity to make the science of orchestration serve formal ends. As a matter of fact the theme is vitiated by harmonic dullness, and the *allegro* is also inclined to hint at harmonic subtlety rather than succeed at it. Too often the chords are ambiguously placed in such a way as to leave us guessing at Berlioz's purpose. They are the crudities which his critics have loved to dwell on and which are rarely to be found outside these early works of adventure.

There is no lack of spirit in this *allegro* and greater conciseness than in the other three overtures of this early period. The themes are thoroughly orchestral, in fact the opening gesture (five bars long) would not ordinarily pass for a theme in the traditional sense. It is mere muscle-stretching, concluding in a stamped out arpeggio, a characteristic rest on the bar line, and an elegant transition to the dominant:

Here we get a theme that brings Italy to mind rather than Scotland, and its later treatment supplies much of the interest of this overture. Its original woodwind shape is:

EX. 2

with the characteristic passionate swelling in an otherwise Rossinian line. Berlioz at once gives it to the violins in *their* manner:

In the coda it is frivolously doubled in pace, and treated to an authentic Rossini *crescendo*:

EX. 4

The most striking passage of the movement opens the lengthy coda. It is one of those eerie moments when Berlioz looses off from the shore of tonality, feels his way forward by chromatic steps, and eventually returns miraculously to land. The upper woodwind hold soft numinous chords over the strings' suggestions of thematic fragments. Off-beat pizzicati dart through the texture. It was a hazardous undertaking for a young man, but a worth-while trial for many greater things to come.

Waverley is a work that neither gets to grips with Scott (*Rob Roy* is no more successful) nor draws out Berlioz's latent powers of dramatic expression. It was useful orchestral training, in fact his first plan was to ask for two flutes, two piccolos, three clarinets, and an unusual body of strings. Its weaknesses are the too impersonal quality of the material, a tendency to apply facile counterpoint, and its harmonic limitations, but I doubt if we should grumble at these shortcomings were it not for the immeasurably greater achievement of the overture to *Les Francs Juges*.

LES FRANCS JUGES

It seems natural to speak of *Waverley* first in spite of Berlioz's avowal that it came later in time, because it is truly a less advanced work. This contrast supports my firm conviction that the *Francs Juges* overture underwent considerable revision before reaching its final form. The autograph is lost, so that the earliest text we have is that of the score published in 1836. Is it possible that the opening *adagio sostenuto* (especially its first twenty and last eight bars) could have been written without a knowledge of Beethoven? The accepted facts are that the overture belongs to 1827, that Habeneck gave the first concert of the Société des Concerts du Conservatoire on 9 March 1828, introducing the *Eroica* to France, and that the *Francs Juges* overture received its first performance some two and a half months later. *Egmont* and *Coriolan* were heard in the course of the year.

It betrays many traits, to be sure, that we observe in other works of Berlioz's youth – the four-square rhythms, the uncertain unisons, the frequent grace notes – but it also displays an elemental force that springs from the subject matter of the opera, and which Berlioz described as 'monstrous, colossal, horrible'. The impressive unison melody in D flat on the brass looks forward to the apocalyptic vision of the *Requiem* (already prefigured in the Mass of 1825), to the intervention of the Prince at the beginning of *Romeo and Juliet*, and, diabolically transformed, to Mephistopheles' 'Invocation' in *The Damnation of Faust*. It stands for Olmerick, the villain-tyrant of the opera, chief of the sinister Vehmgericht, whose deeds darkened the already dark mediaeval German forests. Whether any of the rest of the overture belongs directly to the music of the opera or not we cannot tell. The second subject of the *allegro*, a melody of extraordinary grace and fluency and quite un-Berliozian in its regular periods, was borrowed from a youthful quintet (now lost). The opening of the *allegro* is utterly unvocal in character, symphonic in the manner of Beethoven, and suggestive of some relentless dramatic impulse. The section which most obtrudes in the form of the piece is the bizarre and protracted passage in C minor over which Berlioz, borrowing his teacher Lesueur's predilection for covering his scores with instructions to the players, has written:

> The orchestra here assumes a dual character: the strings must play in rough and violent style, without covering up the flutes. The flutes and clarinets on the other hand play with a sweet and melancholy expression.

The music suggests the emotional disturbance of a placid scene, but the working out is symphonic rather than operatic; the melody may have belonged to the pastoral scenes of the opera, the interjections seem to serve only the overture's purpose.

Once the second subject melody has broken across this strange episode and run its course for the second time, the overture gathers the same extraordinary momentum that we find in the codas of the *Corsair*, *Beatrice and Benedict*, and many other movements. When F major seems finally and triumphantly reached, the heaven-storming strains of Olmerick's trombones break in, answered by the shriek of two *Freischütz*-like piccolos, some bizarre chromatics, and the final affirmation of the tonic.

Not only does it surpass *Waverley* in dramatic imagination, it also occupies a different category of achievement from the half-dozen fragments that have survived of the opera itself, excepting only the 'March of the Guards', later to become the 'March to the Scaffold' in the *Fantastic Symphony*. What went wrong with this project was the inability of the librettist, Berlioz's friend Humbert Ferrand, to complete his share of the task and the poor prospect of any acceptance at the Opéra or at any other theatre. Berlioz not only realised that precious years devoted to an intractable opera were ill-spent; his constant exposure to new *coups de tonnerre* also opened up other channels of expression, leading to the Goethe settings of the *Eight Scenes from Faust*, the Moore settings of the *Irish Melodies*, and finally in 1830 to the *Fantastic Symphony*. The opera was abandoned, but the overture acknowledged.

KING LEAR

Having finally, and at the fourth time of asking, won the coveted Prix de Rome in the summer of 1830, Berlioz reluctantly left Paris at the end of the year for Italy where he was expected to absorb the relics of antiquity and compose music of a comparable classicism. He did neither, and completed very few works of any kind during his stay. He was obliged to submit some compositions to the Institute as evidence of dedication to his art, but he strangely did not submit the best work to come out of this period of two years: the *King Lear* overture. It was written in May 1831 in Nice, and the story of how he wound up there after a great emotional crisis is told in the *Memoirs*. The realisation that his supposed engagement to the flighty Camille Moke was over and that he would not after all be obliged to commit suicide released a flood of creative energy and swept him clean of a deal of accumulated emotional tension. He spent three weeks at Nice which he later described as the three happiest weeks of his life, because his recovery was instantaneous he soon learned that he was not to forfeit his precious pension, and he wrote much music.

He first read Shakespeare's *King Lear* near Florence on the way north, but he had never seen it performed. Berlioz returned constantly to Shakespeare throughout his life not only for his musical works and for frequent allusions in his letters and writings, but also for spiritual company, more and more so as life went on. When setting Shakespeare to music he never adopted the same form twice, so that we have a choral fantasia on *The Tempest* (1830), an overture on *King Lear* (1831), a choral symphony on *Romeo and Juliet* (1839), a funeral march for *Hamlet* (1848), and an opera (*Beatrice and Benedict*) on *Much Ado About Nothing*, as well as indirect settings of Shakespeare in *The Death of Ophelia* and in the great love duet in Act IV of *The Trojans*. In *King Lear* he attempted to compress a play into the smallest frame, which probably accounts for the difficulty we face if we try to approach the music from the Shakespearian standpoint. Furthermore Berlioz offered few hints of any meaning, direct or allusive, to be conveyed by the music. Is the opening theme in the lower strings representative of Lear himself? Is the oboe second subject of the *allegro* a projection of Cordelia? Does the pizzicato chord of G major near the end symbolise something snapping in the deranged king's brain, as Strauss suggested? Or is the overture no more than an 'unmistakably tragic work'?

So far as I am aware, only two references to any precise meanings in the overture were ever made by Berlioz himself. In 1854 the blind king of Hanover heard it and expressed his admiration to Berlioz as follows:

Magnificent, M. Berlioz, magnificent, your orchestra speaks, you have no need of words. I followed every scene: the entrance of the king into the council chamber, the storm on the heath, the terrible prison scene, and the despair of Cordelia. Oh! that Cordelia! How well you have painted her! So tender, so timorous! Heartrending! Beautiful!

Berlioz, usually so quick to relish irony wherever he found it, reproduces this in his *Memoirs* without the slightest indication that the king's perception was anything but right. These things do not seem too literal for Berlioz, even though there still remains the problem of relating the music precisely to the play. There is confirmation in a letter to the Baron von Donop of Brunswick dated 2 October 1858. The Baron had clearly asked how the overture was to be interpreted. Berlioz replied:

Concerning the timpani passage in the *King Lear* overture:

here is my reply: it used to be the custom at the court of Charles X, as late as 1830, to announce the king's entrance into his chambers (after Mass on Sundays) to the sound of an enormous drum which beat a strange rhythm of five beats passed on by tradition from time immemorial. From this I had the idea of accompanying the entry of Lear into his council chamber for the scene of the division of the kingdom by a similar effect on the timpani.

I did not intend his madness to be represented until the middle of the *allegro*, when the basses bring in the theme of the introduction in the middle of the storm.

This gives us a clue; at any rate parts of the overture depict incidents from the play, and it is therefore not too fanciful to allow the imagination to see Cordelia, even the Fool, if one wishes.

But the construction of the work is clear and its tragic mood unmistakable. It opens with a fine, bold statement in recitative. This is later echoed, *pianissimo*, in the violins, ushering in a melody of crystal innocence on the oboe over a gently throbbing pizzicato accompaniment. It is repeated, a little more fully, and then again, in E flat, in a noble transformation on the trombones and horns, before the recitative and Charles X's drumroll announce the entry of the king into his council chamber. The introduction is most impressive and the *allegro* hardly less so, at least it covers up any deficiencies of matter by its vigour and restless energy. It does, too, include two of Berlioz's most gloriously singable melodies in the second subject group. Woodwind solos are rare enough in Berlioz to merit comment, so when the oboe is given two solos in a work of this kind it is tempting to look outside the music for an explanation; possibly there is some programmatic link. Even if not, the oboe is admirably suited to the expressive curve of the melody; the second melody, which grows out of the first, is not particularly Berliozian, but it has the highest breeding:

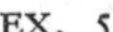
EX. 5

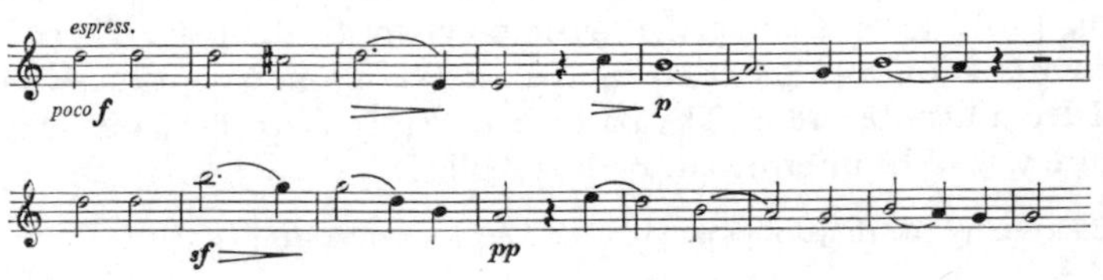

which is greatly intensified when it comes a little later in A minor, and its cadence is suavely harmonised:

EX. 6

A development fragments the material and a recapitulation is proceeding normally when the recitative bursts in in the basses. It then retires for the normal reprise of the second subject melodies before breaking out again and hustling the music into the stormy coda.

In spite of some technical oddities and a certain heavy-handedness in the application of cross-rhythms and link passages, the overture reflects the intensity of conception revealed by a letter:

[On first reading *King Lear*] . . . I uttered a cry of admiration in the face of this work of genius; I thought I would burst from enthusiasm, I rolled around (in the grass, honestly), I rolled convulsively to appease my utter rapture.

Berlioz had not as yet had time to absorb the Italian air that was to penetrate so deeply into his music. *King Lear* lacks the glossy brilliance of all the overtures after *Benvenuto Cellini*, but it has a natural unity and sternness of mind that seem to spring from the spontaneity of its conception.

ROB ROY

Considering that the *Intrata di Rob Roy MacGregor* was sketched immediately after *King Lear*, also in Nice in May 1831, and completed in the mountains of Subiaco the following month, it is astonishingly different in quality. It was performed at the Société des Concerts in Paris in April 1833 and immediately discarded by Berlioz, and the fact that a beautifully neat autograph has survived is nothing to be especially thankful for. Tovey's accusation that Berlioz deliberately preserved scores which he says he burned maligns the sincerity of his self-criticism and overlooks the historical accident that preserved a submission copy in the files of the Institute. Berlioz thought the work 'long and diffuse', and so it is. It should never be performed before an audience who are not wholly aware that Berlioz was ashamed of it.

It is strange, as I have said, that he should have put forward this overture as a sample of his work and not the other. Perhaps he had learnt from the bitter experiences of the Prix de Rome that official taste preferred the commonplace to the inspired. At any rate he can have had few illusions about the relative merit of the two works. *Rob Roy* has one beautiful section for cor anglais solo that was later transferred to the viola in *Harold in Italy* as its principal theme (Ex. 20, p. 40); otherwise it is vacuous and repetitive. Scott, although warmly admired by Berlioz, did not occupy the highest rank in his pantheon; neither here nor in *Waverley* did the best inspiration manifest itself. There is some Scottish colour, with the rhythmic snap, and 'Scots wha' hae' fully in evidence, but the 6/8 rhythms seem determined never to leave the ground; a Caliban-like unison theme in the basses hardly gives the music wings. A second melody was pillaged for *Harold in Italy* and it looks forward to that symphony in some of the rhythmic ideas. *Rob Roy* is poor stuff, comparable in style to the 'Brigands' Chorus' in *Lélio*, the last indisputably weak music Berlioz was to admit to. After the Italian journey these rough-hewn works occur no more, but it is some indication of the turbulence and instability of his condition that his muse still visited him so fitfully.

BENVENUTO CELLINI

On his return from Italy in 1832 Berlioz was above all intent on composing an opera, the quickest avenue to recognition and success, as Meyerbeer's *Robert le Diable* had recently proved. Yet it was some time before he secured satisfactory librettists and any prospect of performance, and even longer (*Harold in Italy* intervened) before he found time (equals money) to settle down to composition. He had chosen Benvenuto Cellini as his subject, and he started work in 1835; the opera finally reached the stage of the Paris Opéra in 1838.

The task of composing an overture to an opera like *Benvenuto*

Cellini was a very different matter from the attempt to translate a play or a novel into instrumental language, so that one should not demand the same formal discipline in what was conventionally a pot-pourri of themes to be heard later; there is no equivalent test of imaginative or literary sensitivity. But Berlioz had absorbed Gluck's precepts of the relevance of the overture to an opera and had poured into the *Francs Juges* overture all the Satanic power that he hoped the opera might have portrayed, had it been completed. *Benvenuto Cellini* was a startlingly different and unexpected opera for an admirer of Gluck and Beethoven, for it was conceived as an *opéra-comique* with spoken dialogue and later given grand opera status without anything being subtracted. It contrasts high seriousness and *buffo* comedy in a manner better known in *Die Meistersinger*, but really more characteristic of Berlioz's methods than of Wagner's.

Benvenuto Cellini is such a cornucopian opera that Berlioz was hardly short of ideas from which to build an overture. His difficulty was to compress the material into manageable shape. In fact he only uses two melodies directly from the opera and one slightly altered. The main *allegro* material is newly devised. This overture establishes Berlioz's now standard pattern of opening with a snatch of the *allegro*, then the slow introduction, followed by a return to the main *allegro*. The very first gesture is a superb call to attention with strong yet elusive cross-rhythms. The slow section is the more effective for one's awareness of the brilliant *allegro* that is to follow, but there is none the less time to linger over the Cardinal's solemn theme (first heard pizzicato in the cellos and basses) and Harlequin's beautiful arietta, somewhat overscored on its second statement. As in *King Lear* the music moves to E flat for a decorated version of the Cardinal's theme, the theme itself striding broadly on the cellos, bassoons, and bass clarinet (a novelty at the time) against flitting figures on the violins and upper woodwind.

The *allegro* goes *con impeto* without the least hindrance. The second subject runs a full twenty bars, and its second statement, on violins and violas in octaves, warms the heart even more than its first. Here is a superb example of Berlioz's melodic gift in full flood, with the basses bouncing in after two bars to maintain the pulse:

x. 7

The working out abounds in teasing cross-rhythms, surprise entries, surprise modulations, breathtaking touches of orchestration, and after a sudden *animato* the inevitable, glorious superimposition of the Cardinal's theme on the *allegro* drives home the peroration.

Benvenuto Cellini is a splendid overture, and it well deserves to be one of the most popular. Tumultuous, tuneful, well balanced, it meets the simple requirements of a curtain-raiser most effectively, while there is great technical subtlety and warmth of feeling for more demanding ears. It even pleased the Opéra audience of 1838. It was the only thing that did, for the mistrust of the artists and the management at that famous première guided the opera towards certain failure. Berlioz's music was altogether too difficult and original and the libretto also offended contemporary notions of what a libretto ought to be. In the case of *Les Francs Juges* the overture gives too flattering an idea of the opera itself; in *Cellini* the overture is not better than the rest – it is a part of it, and a typically impetuous and vital part. The failure of *Cellini* consigned an enormous score to Berlioz's bottom drawer. Five years later he mounted a small salvage operation on some of the more lively music in the opera by putting together a concert overture under the title *Roman Carnival*, since it draws largely on the Carnival scene at the end of the second act. This was first performed in the Salle Herz, Paris, on 3 February 1844.

LE CARNAVAL ROMAIN

The *Roman Carnival* and *Corsair* overtures belong to the years between the *Funeral and Triumphal Symphony* and *The Damnation of Faust* and were both intended as useful concert works, extrovert and rousing. *Roman Carnival* is an orchestral showpiece, very difficult to play but not difficult to make effective. It was put together when Berlioz had just completed his *Treatise on Instrumentation*, which confirmed his reputation as a master of this untaught art. His scores remind us just as forcibly of his instrumental skill. *Roman Carnival* is brilliantly scored, and it is interesting to compare the layout here with that of the original version in the opera. Instruments can chatter in repeated quavers at an *allegro vivace* better than voices can; in fact one would never suspect that the principal themes of the *allegro* were taken from an operatic chorus so delicately and swiftly do the violins and wind pass them back and forth. The cor anglais solo of the slow section is more obviously vocal. In fact it is the duet between Cellini and Teresa in the first act of the opera, and Berlioz develops it by simple restatement. After a dark and mysteriously swelling low G on the clarinet has intervened in the opening *allegro* gestures and prepared for a new key, the melody is stated as simply as possible by the cor anglais in C major. A diminished seventh twists the tonality into E major where the theme is exactly repeated, now in the violas, with a graceful countermelody in the wind and a more lively rhythm in the accompaniment. The next restatement is in A, involving the full orchestra, and not only is the melody answered in canon, one beat distant, by the upper wind and strings; the slow and serene pace of the melody is thrown into sharp relief by the chattering, dancing rhythms underneath. The timpani, triangle, side-drums and brass beckon tantalisingly to the dance. The orchestration is superbly handled, the love duet sailing on in apparent oblivion of the merry-making elsewhere. The duet plays itself out on its own, and then three bars of explosive wizardry – a Ravelian surge of wind chromatics, up and down – land us right in the middle of the carnival.

So fleeting is the pace that we barely notice the regularity of eight-bar sentences. The music trips in and out of remote keys with amazing sleight of hand. Consider the sheer impudence of this snatch of C sharp major in an A major passage:

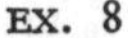

Another fragment appears teasingly at $4\frac{1}{2}$-bar intervals:

EX. 9

The main theme of the *allegro* succeeds this with a heavy crash and accumulates an irresistible momentum, sufficient to carry through a written-out repeat of the *allegro* so far. Remote keys and rhythms then succeed each other more closely, and the music dwindles to a single line on the violins. A chord of B flat jokingly establishes a pedal A over which the love theme of the *andante* enters in a typically Berliozian fugato, that pays heed neither to the length of the theme, nor to the distance and keys of the entries, but concentrates more on building up a strong *crescendo* for the return. This is more of a coda than a recapitulation as the action is swift and cursory. A violent passage in 2/4 precedes the last statement of the dance with the trombones crashing down the scale. Just as one thinks the last chord has arrived a series of overwhelming chords in the brass add a final flourish to the revelries. Strings and percussion leave the last pause to the wind, a simple but stunning effect.

LE CORSAIRE

The next overture, *The Corsair*, was new, even though it is often supposed (wrongly) to date from the same stay in Nice as that which produced *King Lear* and *Rob Roy*. Berlioz returned there in August 1844 after a particularly wearisome series of Paris concerts, and wrote a concert overture. He named it after the prominent stone tower where he lodged and which still stands (suitably emplaqued) overlooking the sea at the end of the Boulevard des Anglais – the 'Tour des Ponchettes' – and the work appeared in a concert on 19 January 1845 under the title 'La Tour de Nice'. Later Berlioz revised it and gave it the name *Le Corsaire Rouge* (after Fenimore Cooper's *The Red Rover*) and finally *Le Corsaire*, the title under which he published it in 1852. It is one of his most spirited and characteristic works, although the general view in the past century has been that it is not one of the better overtures. The multiplicity of titles in fact damages not the music but only possibly Berlioz himself, who might be accused of 'manipulating' his programmes rather than of being inspired by them. The truth is that the work undoubtedly grew from the atmosphere and associations of Nice; this is really its 'inspiration'. But he still had to capture the essence of the music with the most appropriate and evocative literary connotation he could find. He tried Fenimore Cooper; he ended up with Byron, with no special attributions that should send us hunting through the texts. *Any* suggestion of Byron worked wonders for Berlioz's generation, and the deletion of the 'rouge' would have been irresistible. It hardly weakens the spell of the music, which is thoroughly buccaneering and sea-borne from beginning to end. Berlioz's town-bred son Louis never wavered in his determination to go to sea, putting into practice his father's somewhat idealistic longing for distant shores. The *Corsair*, however, is a Mediterranean work, like *Beatrice and Benedict* and *The Trojans*, for it was on the Mediterranean that Berlioz had his first experience of the sea when crossing from Marseilles to Leghorn in 1831. There is more than a memory of that voyage (vividly recounted in the *Memoirs*) in the *Corsair*, and a report of a performance in Weimar in 1856 even claimed that it was actually written during a three-day storm at sea, presumably the same rough passage.

There is another clue in a later description of his preoccupations at Rome:

During the fierce summer heat I used to spend whole days in St Peter's. I took a volume of Byron with me and settled comfortably into a confessional to enjoy the cool atmosphere and the awesome silence . . . I devoured this ardent poetry at my leisure; I followed the Corsair's adventures over the waves; I felt a profound affection for this character at once ruthless and tender, merciless yet generous-hearted, a bizarre compound of two apparently opposite feelings, hatred of mankind and love of a woman.

Revision greatly improved the work, for Berlioz's original plan lacked the long and marvellously beautiful melody in A flat that fills the *adagio sostenuto* section and recurs, artfully speeded up, in the course of the *allegro*, and the coda was also strengthened. It opens with a rushing mighty scale that reminds us of the closing gestures of the first movement of the *Fantastic Symphony* and of the *Benvenuto Cellini* overture, now brilliantly transformed into a surge and billow, answered by teasing syncopations in the wind almost too fast to be properly effective. The *adagio* is ravishing, the melody clamours for words, and even if the last six bars are repeated it is still not enough. Notice Berlioz's obsession with the note of D flat in the basses, a recurrent booming that strangely governs and magnetises the harmony.

The *allegro* reveals Berlioz playing naughtily at un-Berliozian games like canon and inversion, and not giving up, as he often did, after a few bars. The opening theme:

EX. 10

is immediately stated in inversion:

EX. 11

and then in canon, in D flat, the bassoons, ophicleide, and basses thrown lop-sided by the cornets and trombones:

EX. 12

For a second subject this heavy-booted theme is made capricious and dancing and presented in the dominant. Soon there are sighing suggestions of the *adagio* theme over four gruffly stamping bassoons, which then appears *espressivo* in C major, now at the fast pace, but still punctuated by *sforzandos* in the bass.

In the reprise the inversion is forgotten but the canon is more ferocious, and one senses the urgency of the music as it strides boldly into the most infectious and powerful of all Berlioz's powerful codas. The tension comes from the relentless harmonic movement and the constant syncopation (with perhaps a conscious glance towards Beethoven's *Leonora No. 3*), and the grandeur from the long series of declarations in the brass against swirling rising scales in the strings. The final tutti statement of Ex. 10 is vulgar or glorious according to taste, but there is no denying the revelation when after eight bars it lifts itself up a tone into D major. Four bars from the end a *fortissimo* A flat chord reminds us of the *adagio* before plunging on to the final C.

In the *Corsair* Berlioz most successfully solved the problem of integrating his slow and fast sections, much more so than in *Benvenuto Cellini* and *Roman Carnival*, and though its allure is probably less striking, the orchestral magic is more evenly spread and more compulsive. It is a great pity that Berlioz wrote forgettable and forgotten nationalist cantatas like the *Hymne à la France* and *L'Impériale* at a time when he might have been adding to his stock of such overtures – or even writing more operas.

BÉATRICE ET BÉNÉDICT

Of the two operas that Berlioz did write at the end of his career, only one, *Beatrice and Benedict*, bore an overture. The other, *The Trojans*, established a fruitful precedent by plunging straight into the action of Act I without any orchestral preliminaries. Five years after completing the score, when despair of seeing any of it staged compelled him to divide the opera into two, he wrote an orchestral prologue to the second part, *The Trojans at Carthage*, but this is in no sense an overture and it is quite unsuitable for performance as a concert-piece on its own. The overture to *Beatrice and Benedict*, completed after the rest of the opera in 1862, pursues the familiar pattern of the other later overtures, but it is much more of a pot-pourri of the opera's music than that to *Benvenuto Cellini*. This is probably due to the conventions of *opéra-comique*, the French form of dialogue opera, where melodiousness and memorability were prime necessities. Nevertheless Berlioz weaves half a dozen references to the opera into a remarkably coherent and self-sufficient piece, worthy of comparison with any of the other overtures, and in polish, delicacy and grace at least their superior. It is technically the most taxing and the hardest to bring off.

Consider the cross-rhythms of the opening *allegro*, drawn from the opera's finale: within no time at all Berlioz is throwing groups of four across the triple pulse of the bar, and the silences make it no easier to grasp. After the *andante* section the *allegro* returns, not in the triple rhythm we had been led to expect but in a lively *alla breve*. Yet Berlioz is quickly teasing the ear with compound cross-rhythms against the simple metre of the music.

The angularity and pace of the opening phrase, the most important in the overture, is unusual for Berlioz: it represents the wispish nature of love between two beings given passionately to loggerheads:

EX. 13

The dotted figures that accompany this are important and pervade the whole overture. Against this constant agitation and pulse the *andante* acts as an island of tranquillity. It is the melody sung by Beatrice as she recalls the strangely mixed feelings with which she had witnessed Benedict's departure for the wars, and is presented without any elaboration or comment. Echoes of the night-music from the close of Act I – tremolo *divisi* violins, ostinato bass, and an expressionless rising scale in the wind – lead in (by way of a somewhat awkward modulation) to the return of the *allegro*. When the time comes for some new material the strings suddenly rush up the scale in a burst of triplets leaving a void underneath. Into this void steps a rousing march, with plenty of dotted rhythms. A third theme is in the dominant and this has a calmer, steadier demeanour with long notes. The second violins keep mentioning the livelier music, and this eventually takes over and leads back, over a pause, to the recapitulation. Berlioz touches the heights when, as the violins rush upwards for a second time, the march leaps in in a new and surprising key, E flat. He has now assumed his peroration style, even though the coda has not yet been reached. When it comes it has another masterly surprise in store with a quick build-up towards a climactic diminished seventh:

EX. 14

It repeats itself, but this time the trombones have other ideas, with a late unison E flat:

EX. 15

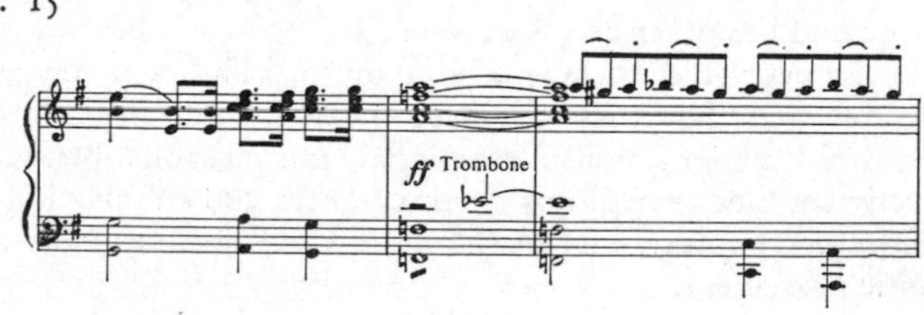

The best opera overtures are by no means those that the concert audience loves best, for the needs of theatre and hall are so different. The *Beatrice and Benedict* overture is more brilliant in the theatre than when detached from its opera, because it seems to suggest and colour much of what is to come. It is a wonderful start to the opera, it encompasses the mood and pace of this witty Shakespearian frolic, yet it has neither the strength nor the glamour to match *Roman Carnival* or *Corsair* on its own. To compare it with *Les Francs Juges* and the other early overtures serves to remind us of how far apart they stand in style and elegance. Early Berlioz is more northern and ponderous, and however assured in characterisation and technique, it shows a superb orchestral style still in the making.

The Symphonies

SYMPHONIE FANTASTIQUE

The *Fantastic Symphony* is at once the most bewildering, the most novel, and the most popular of Berlioz's works. The listener brought up on the symphonies of Beethoven and Brahms, even of Bruckner, must surely scratch his head when confronted with this remarkable work and wonder whether it is really a symphony at all, in the accepted sense of the word. Yet it was Berlioz's very discovery of Beethoven's symphonies that brought the work into being; without this revelation he would doubtless never have written symphonies at all. For until he reached the age of 24 his music was developing rapidly but inconspicuously on the lines of Gluck and the other composers he listened to so keenly at the Opéra – Lesueur (his teacher), Cherubini, Sacchini, and the rest. There followed the years 1827–30, the most turbulent in his career, lived under intense emotional and nervous pressure, productive of much startlingly original music, and culminating in the *Fantastic Symphony*, one of the most vivid documents of the romantic movement.

It probably never occurred to the ardent spirits of literary romanticism, drunk on the heady wine of Schiller, Géricault or Hugo, that the art of Haydn and Mozart could blazon the new message. Romanticism was essentially a literary movement, it thrived on pictorial and poetic images of a kind altogether too daring and fantastic for eighteenth-century minds. Yet it was music's very inability to depict objects and ideas with precision that lent it so powerfully to the new expression. The infinite, the unimaginable, the human soul itself – these were not to be encompassed in any medium so forcibly as in music, with its unequalled capacity for suggestion, for association, and for plumbing the uncharted depths of the spirit. The favourite subject-matter – hopeless love, uncontrollable passion, unattainable femininity, despair, death, nightmares and supernatural powers – and the new insistence upon the artist's impulsive involvement, on inspiration – these appeared most forcibly for the first time in music in the *Fantastic Symphony*. At one blow music was revealed as itself an intrinsically romantic art, as *the* romantic art.

Berlioz was in 1827 a highly sensitive man subjected to a series of powerful external impressions that intensified the activity of his already fervid imagination. The first of these thunder blows, and the most violent, was the visit to Paris of an English theatrical troupe that included Kemble, Keen, and Macready. In September of that year they gave a series of Shakespeare performances at the Odéon Theatre that electrified the whole circle of passionate young men who were to speak for their generation, Hugo, de Vigny, Gautier, Dumas, Nerval, Delacroix and Berlioz. The one musician in this circle shared their unbounded admiration for Shakespeare, and was even more passionate than they in delirious adoration of the principal actress, Harriet Smithson, whose Irish inflections were said to have vitiated her complete success in London. He roamed the streets, he tells us in his *Memoirs*, in a state of delirium, barely summoning the courage to return to the theatre for a second or third assault upon his sensibilities. At the time, it seems, the personal impression was predominant. The discovery of Shakespeare worked itself out more slowly and with more profound consequences for his music.

This double impact was soon followed by two more: first the reading of Gérard de Nerval's translation of Goethe's *Faust*, and soon afterwards the first performance in France of the *Eroica* Symphony in March 1828 at the Conservatoire. Settings of Goethe obsessed him for a full year. We hear of a *Faust* symphony and a *Faust* ballet, but only a set of *Eight Scenes from Faust*, the kernel of the later *Damnation of Faust*, were completed. He read Thomas Moore's *Irish Melodies* and set nine of them in the summer of 1829. By the spring of 1830 his passion for Harriet Smithson had turned sour, disillusioned by her cold response, and a new work took sudden shape as if from the realisation that the whole experience could be enveloped in the outlines of a Beethoven symphony. This flash of insight brought into being a work of undying fascination and popularity, and a cornerstone in musical history. The first performance of the *Fantastic Symphony* was given at the Paris Conservatoire on 5 December 1830.

Not all the music was new when the symphony was composed. At many points he utilised existing material where it seemed to fit his dramatic and symphonic scheme. The symphony is a drama; the burning novelty was the working out of an explicit personal experience as a drama in five movements. Hence the true title: *Episode in the Life of an Artist*. As it inhabits the world of fantasy and dreams it bears the subtitle *Fantastic Symphony*. Unity is imposed by the identity of the artist and by the use of a theme, which Berlioz described as the *idée fixe*, that recurs in different guises in all five movements. The transformations of this theme, a new use of a very old device (not to mention Berlioz's recurrent technique of transforming one theme into another), passed through Liszt into the common stock of late nineteenth-century techniques, and we can see why it proved so useful. It creates diversity within unity; the theme is the same yet different; in this case the beloved is the same object seen by the artist against different backgrounds and in different states of mind.

From Beethoven's *Pastoral* Symphony Berlioz borrowed and extended the idea of supplying descriptive programmes for each movement. When the score was published in 1846 Berlioz said that the detailed programme need not always be circulated to the audience, but that the titles of the movements would suffice. He hoped that the music would offer sufficient interest on its own account. This claim is not quite true, for by no means everything in the score is self-explanatory. Composers do occasionally suffer from bad consciences when they make their music too explicit, and Beethoven tried to worm his way out of having depicted nightingales, cuckoos and quails by saying it was the expression of feeling, which it clearly is not. Mahler, too, was embarrassed by the programme of his First Symphony. Without the programme of the *Fantastic Symphony* the close of the 'March to the Scaffold', the distant thunder in the 'Scene in the Country', and much of the 'Witches' Sabbath', including the 'Dies irae' plain-chant, are incomprehensible. Berlioz's text makes all this plain, besides supplying us with a direct and valuable insight into the workings of his imagination; we may not like Berlioz's interpretation of the notes, but it is at least his; it too forms an episode in the artist's life.

A young musician of morbid disposition and powerful imagination poisons himself with opium in an attack of despairing passion. The dose of the drug, too weak to kill him, plunges him into a deep sleep accompanied by strange dreams in which sensations, feelings and memories are transformed in his sick brain into musical images and ideas. The beloved herself appears to him as a melody, like an *idée fixe*, an obsessive idea that he keeps hearing wherever he goes.

In Berlioz's original version only the last two movements were literally 'fantastic', concerned with the realm of opium-induced dreams. His interest in opium dreams came from reading de Musset's translation of De Quincy's *Confessions of an English Opium Eater,* but he himself never found other than medical or sensational uses for opium.

The first movement is headed 'Reveries, Passions':

He first recalls the sickness of the soul, the flux of passion, the unaccountable joys and sorrows he experienced before he saw his beloved; then the volcanic love that she suddenly inspired in him, his delirious raptures, his jealous fury, his persistent tenderness, his religious consolations.

The opening slow introduction to the movement appropriately expresses the artist's earlier state of mind by using a melody of his youth, once a setting of Florian's 'Je vais donc quitter pour jamais'. Muted violins breathe a fresh, young passion, and harmony and scoring are applied with extraordinary originality and skill. There are enough ideas in this introduction alone to serve a full symphonic movement, and one might well claim that Chateaubriand's *vague des passions* was nowhere else so evocatively expressed. One is loath to embark on the *allegro*, but the *idée fixe* presents itself forcefully on violins and first flute, unaccompanied save for some irregular spasms in the lower strings. The contrast of passionate legato and gruff angularity is deliberate, and though we may not admire the melody as a beautiful entity in its own right (Berlioz did not intend that we should), the rise and fall of the phrases, the violent expression marks, and the insidious chromaticisms perfectly serve his purpose. The *idée fixe* appears in the Prix de Rome cantata of 1828, *Herminie*, but the melody may well have come into being under the direct impact of Miss Smithson the previous autumn:

EX. 16

The form of the movement has little in common with classical sonata form; Berlioz was more concerned with the working out of a musical idea according to its lights than in forcing the music into formal strait-jackets. There is a repeated exposition but no second subject, only a kind of pendant theme which veers towards E minor:

EX. 17

There is a recapitulation but scarcely any formal development. There is a series of codas that occupy nearly half the movement. Berlioz is anxious to give the impression that the melodic fragments, particularly those based on the six first notes of the *idée fixe*, are not subjected to systematic discussion and elaboration so much as representing a constant, shifting presence that makes itself felt; they are the governors not the victims of the music's progress. There is much in the movement that hangs only loosely in its frame, yet critics from Schumann onwards have insisted upon its intellectual coherence and its taut discipline of detail. Twice in Schumann's pioneering essay on the symphony does the expression 'in spite of the apparent formlessness of the work . . .' occur, each time pointing to the originality and sense of the musical order rather than to its compliance with accepted formal standards. There are strokes of real inspiration, of which the most memorable are the oboe theme that rises like Aphrodite out of the grumblings of the *idée fixe*; the overpowering return of the melody in C major on the cornets; but not (let us be honest) the *religioso* chords that round the movement off.

The second movement, 'A Ball', is dramatically and musically crystal clear, so too is the orchestration, with two harps, no bassoons, and just one oboe. The dance melody is deliberately unsophisticated, which is why Berlioz varies the accompaniment whenever it returns. We recognise a more personal presence in the second idea, which shares the same contours and impulsive expression marks as Ex. 17:

EX. 18

When the *idée fixe* itself appears, the artist's sudden consciousness of her presence shuts off all awareness of the dance music, the key changes abruptly, and the melody gracefully unfolds in the flute and oboe. Gradually the waltz returns, and after a second appearance of the *idée fixe*, even more detached this time, another of Berlioz's brilliant codas closes the movement.

The slow movement is a 'Scene in the Country', and the debt to Beethoven's *Pastoral* is here most obvious. After the slow introduction of the opening movement, the relationship between imaginative idea and musical working out is more satisfying here than anywhere else in the symphony. It is a wonderfully designed *adagio* and the poetic imagery matches the musical expression at every point: the shepherds' pipes answering one another across the void, the calm of a summer evening in the country, the artist's passionate melancholy, the wind caressing the trees, the agitation caused by the beloved's appearance leading to the brink of despair, the setting sun, the echo of distant thunder, 'solitude . . . silence'. The programme never jars with the form, the melody develops at its natural pace, and the whole has a satisfying symmetry not unlike that of the 'Royal Hunt and Storm', another outdoor movement containing extremes of calm and tempest.

So far Berlioz's imagination has inhabited the world of passionate melancholy and longing, but it now plunges into the depths of the macabre. The fascination of death and horror and the morbid power of supernatural things take over, leaving far behind the language of Beethoven and Gluck. Music had never ventured into this strange territory before. The artist dreams he has killed his beloved, for which he is condemned to death and led to execution.

> The procession moves forward to the sound of a march sometimes dark and sinister, sometimes brilliant and ceremonious, while a heavy tread persists through the clamour. At the end the *idée fixe* reappears for a moment like a last memory of love before being cut short by the fatal blow.

The 'March to the Scaffold', the first and most vividly descriptive of Berlioz's marches, was drawn from the unfinished opera *Les Francs Juges* where it could hardly have had the imaginative impact that it has here. *Bouché* horns, *divisi* double basses, a double pair of timpani, and a relentless rhythm build up a terrifying picture, and the utter nullity of the descending scale, which the cellos and basses play as though it were a theme, contributes to the nightmare. After the double bar the energy of the march increases; one hears the bloodlust of the crowd in the trombones' snarling pedals and the barking strings, and an inexorable dotted rhythm leads to the stark juxtaposition of G minor chords (strings) and D flat major (wind). This is the extreme of horror and derangement, and the tension of the clarinet's *idée fixe*, as a last memory registers piercingly in the brain, is released by the falling blade and a series of bloodthirsty major chords.

Finally, in the 'Dream of a Witches' Sabbath', the artist sees himself beyond the grave, the spectator of a sinister gathering of spectres, monsters, and weird, infernal, mocking creatures. The imagination is king, and the more bizarre the ideas the more effective is the depiction. Inconsequence and oddity become sources of musical virtue, at least in the introductory section of the movement, so that the effect of the beloved's arrival, distorted and grotesque on the E flat clarinet, is this time to impose some semblance of order on the music rather than to disrupt it. The immediate impression is of a scene of chaos and a Bosch-like profusion of ungainly figures, as though at the opening of a sinister black ritual.

When bells toll and the 'Dies irae' bursts forth on bassoons and ophicleides (the ugliest noise Berlioz knew how to make) the ritual is under way. It is followed by the infernal round-dance, not just witches but a 'diabolical orgy' presented as a nervous fugato, and at this point the musician in Berlioz takes over. The material is expounded, chromatically developed and recapitulated in a triumphant blaze when the 'Dies irae' thunders in against the headlong whirl of the dance. Berlioz always has something in reserve for his codas. They drive inexorably to the finish as well as throwing out new ideas. The chipping 'col legno' and trills are succeeded by riotous chromatics on the wind. Once he knows that sooner or later the brass *fortissimo* will descend, how can the listener draw breath?

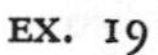

On the final chord of the symphony the timpani do not roll, leaving the air clear for the strident C major of the brass.

There is hardly any aspect of the symphony where Berlioz does not tread new ground, whether in the ground plan of five movements, in the unconventional patterns of each movement, in the importance of the semi-autobiographical programme, in the uncanny translation into sound of mental images, in the resourcefulness of the instrumentation, or in the still striking modernity of his sense of colour. It is uncontrollably, exuberantly youthful, extravagantly conceived, yet instinctively musical. The orchestra is exploited in an altogether revolutionary way; it is not simply that Berlioz asks for two harps, a cor anglais, an E flat clarinet, two ophicleides, four timpani, and a large array of percussion, and expects every instrument to execute things never dreamed of before; he differs from the classical masters in his entirely functional use of individual voices and his creation of orchestral sound by the expert piecing together of timbres, registers, and dynamics.

It is a strange axiom of musical history that the decisive forward strides are usually taken by men of genius, not by inventive cranks. The *Fantastic Symphony* is not important merely because of its astonishing breakthrough into uncharted worlds of symphonic thought, nor because of its disclosure of a whole new instrumental language. Its real value is its capacity to communicate the white-hot fervour of Berlioz's mind, and to renew its multi-dimensional vision at every hearing.

The *Episode* had two sequels, one musical, one biographical. After its first performance Berlioz reluctantly proceeded to Italy to fulfil the terms of the Prix de Rome pension and there wrote *The Return to Life* in which the artist, now named Lélio, recovers from his traumatic experiences and comes to terms with life largely through the healing power of music. The *idée fixe* leaves a lingering question mark at the end of a series of pieces which by no means constitute a symphony, even though they have a loose musical continuity. By using singers and an actor Berlioz breaks with the symphonic, orchestral mode of thought of the *Fantastic Symphony*, and it must inevitably represent a lower level of endeavour, simply because it does not attempt the formal or imaginative designs of the symphony. *Lélio* is a curious and beautiful work, which must on no account be condemned for being six linked works. Berlioz was fond of miscellanies like the *Eight Scenes from Faust*, the nine songs of the *Irish Melodies*, and the three component movements of *Tristia*, and *Lélio* is another of these.

HAROLD EN ITALIE

In life Berlioz persisted in his pursuit of Harriet Smithson, contrived an introduction in 1832 on his return from Italy, and persuaded her to marry him the following year. For the rest of his life she remained for him the embodiment of Ophelia, Juliet, or Desdemona, an idealisation which helped him to surmount for a while the difficulties of an unpropitious partnership. It was in the first happy year of their marriage that he wrote his second symphony, *Harold in Italy*, which is a truer sequel to the *Fantastic Symphony*, in the sense of being representative of his artistic development, than *Lélio*. Once again it sprang from a single linking idea giving shape to a number of impressions gathered in the preceding two or three years, only this time the catalyst was external. Paganini asked Berlioz for a work in which he could display his powers on a fine Stradivarius viola, and obviously had in mind a concerto; but he never in fact played the solo part, finding the first movement 'too full of rests'. He was later handsomely reconciled to the work, as a gift to Berlioz of 20,000 francs betokened, making him the instigator of yet another symphony.

Although relatively few compositions were completed during Berlioz's stay in Italy, his powers of invention had not declined or been diverted. Many ideas, including some noted down in connection with a proposed large-scale work about Napoleon's triumphant journey along the same homeward route across the Alps, went into *Harold in Italy*. The music was related to the last hours of Mary Queen of Scots before it became associated with Byron's Childe Harold, the most popular literary character of the day. This indecision about the subject-matter does not diminish the force of the music's portrayal of Harold, but it is a striking weakness after the unswerving vision of the *Fantastic Symphony*. Indeed it is altogether a much less startling, original, or progressive work, beautiful and expressive though the music is. It may perhaps cause surprise that the supposedly revolutionary young

Berlioz was so conventional as to write a symphony in four movements, to insert mere pictorial titles at the head of each in place of the more dramatic programme of the *Fantastic Symphony*, to have a first movement form closer to sonata form, and to borrow from the Choral Symphony with little modification the device of recalling each of the three preceding movements in turn before striking out on the last, the 'Brigands' Orgy'. *Harold* is a less revolutionary and fiery work, even though certain features are both novel and far-sighted. The idea of a solo instrument in such a symphony was new; and the choice of viola was unusual; given that the instrument was dictated by Paganini's wishes, it aroused Berlioz's instant sympathy since it possessed the same dark, melancholy, 'romantic' colour that also endeared the cor anglais to him as a solo instrument, but it would be false to pretend that Berlioz solved the problems of concert-hall balance between soloist and orchestra. What he does establish is the personality of the instrument, portraying the thoughts and impressions generated in a sensitive observer (Harold, alias Berlioz himself) by scenes of a romantic nature.

Mountains, pilgrims, bells, and brigands were as much the standard appurtenances of the literature and art of that generation as the witches and diabolism of the first symphony. Only, whereas the first sprang from experience projected into the imagination, in the second symphony the experience is less personal and less artfully presented. Berlioz had at least come across pilgrims and brigands in Italy, even if he had perhaps not participated in any orgies. Although the pictorial evocations of the symphony are scarcely more elaborate than those of Mendelssohn's *Italian* Symphony, the background is richly filled in by the chapters of the *Memoirs* devoted to his stay in Italy – indispensable reading for a proper understanding of *Harold in Italy*.

An *idée fixe* again recurs in each movement, usually as an identification of Harold himself, but by no means always. The characterisation is shared between the theme, the solo viola, and the orchestra. The theme is unusually simple and symmetrical in its first part:

EX. 20

Yet it soon generates more characteristic ramifications. It has been usefully pointed out that unlike the *idée fixe* of the *Fantastic Symphony*, which keeps reappearing in different guises, here in *Harold* the theme remains unaltered by its recurrence in the four movements. Harold is a more detached observer than the passionate and desperately involved artist of four years earlier. The fact that the movements are given curt titles rather than extended patterns of action also creates a less volatile and fleeting impression.

There is one respect in which *Harold in Italy* reaches an extreme point in Berlioz's entire output: rhythm. It is almost a study in rhythm. The *Fantastic Symphony* gave plenty of evidence of Berlioz's rhythmic resource, but here it goes much further, further than he was to go again. Brahms's passion for cross-rhythms is foreshadowed in every movement. There is the whimsical play between viola and bassoon in the first *allegro*:

EX. 21

surrounded by constant 9/8 rhythms drawn across the 6/8 time signature. The fugato is started by the double basses at three notes to a pulse, the cellos enter at four notes, followed by the violas at six notes, and over it all the second subject is thrown in out of phase:

EX. 22

In the 'Pilgrims' March' the tolling bells sound across a pattern created by superimposing 3+4 (wind) over 4+3 (strings) and a *tour de force* is reached in the 'Serenade', the third movement, where the two principal sections combine simultaneously under the watchful eye of Harold's own theme:

EX. 23

The last movement is as taut as a bow-string, and its theme is more distinctive in rhythm than as a melodic contour:

EX. 24

The pulse is constantly switching to 3/2 against the 4/4 bar-lines, and towards the end there is a series of octave jumps in 3/4 only shortly before the whole bar is divided in triplet minims for a final chromatic scale in contrary motion. Berlioz seems to be fighting a prolonged private battle with the bar-line.

This strictly compositional aspect of the work should commend it to those who have little taste for the literary trappings of Berlioz's symphonies. Furthermore there are only a few pictorial elements which depend heavily upon the correct associations. There is little chance of mistaking the intensely melancholy character of the opening fugato of the first movement, with a solo bassoon winding downwards towards the basses. Harold's theme is foreshadowed darkly in the minor and then it enters in the major deprived of its shifting undercurrent and supported thinly by a harp and later two clarinets. After a canonic restatement, with some important touches on the triangle, the movement settles down ('happiness and joy'), its first theme presented in fragments by the orchestra, then whole by the solo viola. Once again Berlioz maintains the pretence of sonata form as far as the double bar and beyond, but seems most at his ease in the later stages of the movement when he can treat the form more freely. There is a lot of genuinely symphonic discussion and the second theme serves its classic duty of providing a strong contrast, with Harold's theme later thrown in with the musical argument.

The 'Pilgrims' March' is more of a period piece. In 1834 such things were still not the commonplace genre piece they were later to become, and there is great skill in the writing. It belongs to a type later known as a 'patrol', with the procession of pilgrims approaching from the distance, passing, and continuing on its way. The melody of the march varies itself subtly, reaching higher and higher at every turn, punctuated by two tolling bells, one on horn and harp, the other nearly two octaves higher on flute, oboe and harp; this is a haunting effect, especially when it moves into the distance. The movement encloses a placid chorale decorated by the viola with arpeggios *sul ponticello* while the march continues unbroken in the bass line.

In the 'Serenade' again interesting and picturesque scenes are lovingly witnessed and recollected. The Abruzzi highlander plays to his mistress on his pipe in the perky rhythm associated with the *pifferari*, then sings his serenade (on the cor anglais) at a more languorous tempo. After the viola has chanted Harold's theme it spreads into some beautiful lyrical phrases which Paganini would never have been ashamed to play. Berlioz, true to his favourite contrapuntal device, brings both rhythms back together, and the movement closes in the clearest C major. With a crash the finale leaps in and the main material of the work is reviewed, not in its proper order, each broken off by violent interjections from the brigands before they start on their orgy. The device is delightfully self-conscious, but it is difficult to establish any compelling psychological justification for its use, except that Beethoven's Choral Symphony was as fine a model as Berlioz knew. We are not aware of any strong nostalgia until much later in the movement when, after the orgy has got under way, with its rumbustious energy, demoniac laughter and flashes of tenderness, Harold re-appears and comments briefly but with inexpressible depth of feeling on the distant echoes of the 'Pilgrims' March'. Soon the rhythms tighten, the strings bestir themselves, and the last phase of the orgy crashes about his ears.

ROMÉO ET JULIETTE

Two major works occupied Berlioz before he wrote another symphony, and both greatly widened his horizons. The first was the opera *Benvenuto Cellini*, which was not staged until after the composition and performance of the other, the *Requiem* of 1837. If it was partly the official recognition awarded to the *Requiem* that opened the doors of the Opéra in 1838, the disastrous reception there of *Cellini* closed them again. Berlioz was more and more isolated from fashionable tastes yet ever more deeply conscious of his own powers and his incapacity to put them to full use. The *Requiem* gratified his passion for music of a grandly ceremonial kind; *Cellini* gratified his passion for the stage and drew from him a score of incredible richness and diversity. Its failure did not in fact deter him from opera, as is so often supposed; there were a number of short-lived projects in the next few years, of which *La Nonne Sanglante* came nearest to completion in the mid-1840s. It was this failure, the failure to find a librettist with whom he could collaborate successfully and his dissatisfaction with the music that Scribe's text elicited, that closed his mind to opera for ten years. After *Cellini* he knew he had it in himself to compose opera and still hoped to prove it.

These projects may help to convince the sceptic that when on 17 December 1838 Paganini presented Berlioz with the famous 20,000 francs he did not immediately write *Romeo and Juliet* as a kind of substitute opera. It was always conceived as a symphony against the background of concurrent (but much less enticing) projects of operas also to be written. The composition of it gave Berlioz intense delight, freed as he was from the enforced distraction of having to earn his living as a critic:

During those seven months how ardently I lived! How boldly I swam in that great ocean of poetry, caressed by the capricious breeze of fancy, beneath the warm rays of that sun of love which Shakespeare kindled, and confident of my power to reach the magic isle where stands the temple of pure art!

The whole symphony was completed by September 1839 and first performed on 24 November of that year; one member of the audience, Richard Wagner, was to learn more than a little from it, although the plan of the work, a large-scale choral symphony, with three soloists and some lengthy movements for the orchestra alone, probably appealed as little to him as it has to symphonic purists. Berlioz's own convictions about the plan and proportions of the symphony were unassailable, deriving from a dozen years of passionate admiration for Shakespeare. In his collection of articles published in 1862 under the title *A Travers Chants* Berlioz discusses a number of settings of *Romeo and Juliet*, including operas by Bellini, Steibelt, Dalayrac and Zingarelli; he clearly did not approach his subject at all casually.

Romeo and Juliet reflects an extraordinary advance on the first two symphonies. It is much longer and larger in scope. It can be approximately schematised as three symphonic movements (an *allegro* with slow introduction, an *adagio*, and a scherzo) followed by two dramatic tableaux, the whole preceded by a vocal prologue and concluded by an extended vocal finale. Berlioz's instrumental skill is less daring but more assured and he has moved far enough away from conventional symphonic patterns to be no longer troubled by them; he no longer seems to suffer from a 'sonata conscience'. To replace the traditional formal devices he developed his own procedures, such as the use of descriptive motives transformed according to context, but without the rigour of the *Leitmotiv* system. In *Harold in Italy*, for example, he borrowed Beethoven's device of thematic reminiscence in a more or less undisguised form. The leap from there to the extraordinary interpenetration of thematic material that we find in *Romeo and Juliet* is very striking. For not only does the 'Tomb Scene' work out earlier thematic motives to an explicit dramatic purpose, we also find the idea reversed in the Prologue. In *Harold* two themes had been pieced together or at least foreshadowed, but here not only are suggestions of melody for the coming symphony adumbrated in advance, the course of the dramatic working out is also put forward in summary form. The Prologue gives a compressed account of the whole action. The nearest precedent is really Beethoven's *Grosse Fuge,* even though that is not likely to have been in Berlioz's mind.

The Prologue is a complex pattern of movement and action. In the central movements Berlioz is about to dispense with voices and enter the inner world of the lovers' tragic passion. Before he does so, the scene has to be set. In a sense there is a conflict between his wish to externalise the drama by adding operatic trappings to a symphonic nucleus and his overriding belief that the central tragedy was beyond the crudities of words and scenery. However, these two impulses stand in clear and wholly satisfactory relation to each other. The prologue and the finale are near the surface. It is necessary to pass through them in order to penetrate to the next ring of thought and action. The whole work is a spiritual journey and its form pursues the dictates not only of Shakespeare's play but also of the different levels at which Berlioz chose to interpret it. The voice and presence of Friar Laurence draw us out from the imagination's holy of holies and lead us back to the real world of Montagues and Capulets.

Berlioz is perfectly explicit about the nature of the work in his preface to the score:

> The genre of this work will surely not be mistaken[1] . . . It is neither a concert opera nor a cantata, but a choral symphony.

The vocal Prologue, he says, is designed to prepare the mind for the orchestral scenes that follow. It tells the complete story in microcosm. A fiery fugato in B minor presents the warring families with its constant flashing cut and thrust, and after a swift build-up the music receives great stabs of pulse from the off-beat double basses. The intervention of the Prince is presented in sombre recitative by the trombones, ophicleide and horns, and at first they transform the fugato:

[1] Mistranslated by the Editor of the Eulenburg miniature score as: 'There is no doubt that the special character of this work will be misunderstood'. This version is equally characteristic of Berlioz' irony, and has turned out to be more accurate.

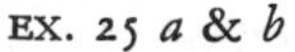

After the Prince's decree the scattering bands of 'rebellious subjects, enemies to peace' are graphically shown dispersing with barely concealed rancour.

A semi-chorus of thirteen voices opens the prologue proper, setting the scene in recitative. A solo contralto is given the delicate task of introducing the two lovers by name, 'Juliet' being especially singled out for hallowed expression. At the mention of the sounds of revelry we hear a foretaste of the 'Ball Scene' and of the altered melody in 6/8, the melody which we are later to hear as the Capulets make their way home from the ball. Romeo's sighs and the lovers' awakened passion are also pre-echoed, at which point the contralto sings the *strophes* 'Premiers transports'. The method is exactly that of the Bach Passions, with contemplative aria breaking into the narrative and expanding the cold statement of recitative in lyric form. It is sufficiently detached to mention Shakespeare by name, an allusion that seems strangely self-conscious, leading as it does to the melodic climax of the song. The second verse is beautifully decorated by the cellos' counterpoint.

Romeo's romantic pallor sets his friends laughing. Mercutio suggests he has been visited by Queen Mab, the dream fairy, and here Shakespeare's lines inspire a magical scherzetto. Pizzicato cellos do the galloping, with flute and piccolo dancing in between the vocal phrases and the chorus's breathless echoes. It is not a redundant 'Queen Mab' scherzo, but a vocal suggestion of the fully developed scherzo that is coming later; the closing bars are identical in both. The summarising Prologue pursues the drama further towards its dénouement by hinting at the sovereign force of death and the final reconciliation of Montagues and Capulets. In the background sounds the monotone of Juliet's funeral music, and the chorus touches on the fugato from the same section.

At this point Berlioz abandons the support of words and embarks on the central matter of the symphony. The movement that follows depicts 'Romeo alone – Melancholy – Concert and Ball – Festivities at the Capulets'. We are at once face to face with the problem of relating Berlioz to Shakespeare, for in the play Romeo sees Juliet for the first time at the Capulets' ball; here, in Berlioz, his lovelorn melancholy precedes the festivity. Later in the score Berlioz was helpful enough to tell us that a knowledge of Garrick's acting version of the play would help the listener. Yet few of the baffled critics of *Romeo and Juliet* in the century after its composition bothered to take the hint until Roger Fiske discovered that Garrick holds the key to more than just the tomb scene. It was Garrick's version that Berlioz saw acted at the Odéon in 1827, and it is extremely unlikely that Harriet Smithson ever performed the authentic one. It is Garrick's sequence, not Shakespeare's, that shaped much of the Symphony. When Berlioz decided to set the reconciliation scene as a finale, omitted by Garrick, he felt impelled to draw attention to the fact, almost in self-justification, in his preface:

> This scene has never been performed on any stage since the time of Shakespeare. But it is too fine, too musical, and it crowns a work such as this too fittingly for a composer to consider any other [viz. Garrick's] treatment.

The rewriting suppressed Romeo's original love for Rosaline, so that Romeo is from his first entry in love with Juliet. Hence Mercutio's jests, which in Shakespeare refer to Rosaline but in Berlioz to Juliet. Hence the melancholy *andante* before the *allegro*, a satisfying symphonic arrangement on Beethoven's pattern, already proven in his first two symphonies. Romeo alone is simply depicted by a long unaccompanied melody for the first violins. This may seem naive, but Berlioz's purpose in withdrawing all but the barest harmonisation is to emphasise the expressive value of every note. It is the *tristesse* he is after. The melody is much more chromatic than is usual in Berlioz, and every inflexion and every interval stands out boldly. In the 'Scene in the Country' the melody was stated in a similar way; here the force of expressive melody in its own right is stronger than ever.

A new melody appears, equally long and expressive, but now

less chromatic and harmonised with a broad, swaying bass line, and this too passes into another melody split between pairs of woodwind. Its triplets, picked up from the previous cadence, conclude with a four-square phrase that might almost come from the Bellini whose *I Montecchi ed i Capuletti* he so despised:

EX. 26

The span of the whole *andante* recalls something of the 'Reveries' music of the *Fantastic Symphony*, and one may well feel reluctant to arrive so soon at the *allegro*. Distant tambourines announce the ball, but in fact we are not plunged straight into the whirl. Romeo's thoughts are still elsewhere, and a solo oboe presents yet another melody of incredible breadth and beauty, later to be superimposed triumphantly on the ball music as if to declare the overriding supremacy of Romeo's passion. The scene is unmistakably vivacious, and the rhythms of the dance are sneakingly reminiscent of the 'Brigands' Orgy'. The *Réunion des deux thèmes* arrives quickly and most of the movement is devoted to an extended coda.

The slow movement, the 'Love Scene' that follows, is justly the most famous part of the work, and the music which Berlioz himself felt most deeply for; he came to regard it as his greatest single achievement. It constantly recurred in his concert programmes; the melody was inscribed in countless albums; for Berlioz it represented the deepest imaginable expression of human emotion. It is the core of the symphony. We have penetrated to the heart of the subject and in this innermost sanctum the language of words and voices has no place. Berlioz makes no apology for not personifying his protagonists; his reasons for not doing so were threefold: (1) he is writing a symphony, not an opera; (2) the scene had been set vocally many times before and he wanted to try something different; (3) the most important:

> The very sublimity of this love made its depiction by the musician so dangerous a task that he has had to give his imagination freer rein than sung words would have allowed, and to have recourse to the language of instruments, a language richer, more diverse, more flexible, and by its very indefiniteness incomparably more powerful.

It is a long movement, rich in melody and atmospheric design, with the sublime calm of the 'blessed, blessed night' interspersed with more agitated sections, the swing from serenity to palpitation and back providing the formal movement. Berlioz's inspiration takes wing the moment he is immersed in the scene. When writing *The Trojans* in 1856 he looked back at the fervour of the experience of composing this scene and recalled that he could barely summon up the iron discipline required to master material of such enervating intensity.

The *adagio* is preceded by some scattered fragments sung by the departing Capulets over slow, still harmonies. The vocal lines are tuneful but unable quite to generate their proper pace, and the effect is of a deadening hand. The tra-la-las ironically cast a tragic shadow over the coming love scene. At first it is not by melody that Berlioz casts his spell but by a murmuring string texture, a rich inner glow of muted violas and divided cellos with alternating commentary from the violins and double-basses, and an occasional sigh from the wind. A slight increase in speed introduces the declaration of passion on the cellos and horns:

EX. 27

The other melodies of the movement draw on this line for their source, particularly the rising three notes, and the effortless expansion of one melody into the next proceeds by a kind of free variation. Absurd though many programmatic interpretations of this movement have been, it is not too fanciful to hear the lovers' rapt exchanges in the alternations of melodic fragments from one instrument to another, and in a brief passage of cello recitative Berlioz almost lapses into the declamatory vocal style he was at pains to avoid. The final statement of the melody is put haltingly together, as at the close of the song 'La Captive', and the fading farewells are beautifully suggested by a repeated cadence ('a thousand times goodnight') which shows Berlioz as unwilling to close the scene as Romeo and Juliet are to part.

In 1854 Berlioz had occasion to compare the slow movements of the *Fantastic Symphony* and *Romeo and Juliet* in the following terms:

In one [*Romeo*] is expressed a southern, Mediterranean love, an Italian sky and a starry night. In the other you will recognise the desolate, feverish northern love, the sombre threats of a stormy horizon on a summer's evening when clouds shoot forth silent lightning flashes. In one it is love in the *presence* of the beloved, in the other it is love that clamours to all nature for the lost beloved. How naive I am to tell you this.

The 'Queen Mab' scherzo fits more obviously into the symphonic than the dramatic framework and its internal form follows the traditional ternary pattern. It takes us away from the lovers and away from Verona. The Queen of Dreams

gallops night by night
Through lovers' brains, and then they dream of love.

The music is Berlioz's supreme exercise in light orchestral texture, a brilliant, gossamer fabric, *prestissimo* and *pianissimo* almost without pause. Even in the trio with its lumbering theme on flute and cor anglais the violas maintain the fairy tread and the violin harmonics hang like dew over the surface of the music. The scherzo swiftly returns and with it a new virtuoso passage for the horns, Queen Mab's 'chariot in an empty hazel-nut', crossed by booms of the bass drum, rare low notes in a high-pitched movement, and rising to the one sudden climax. The sounds become more ethereal and fairylike, low clarinet, high harps and the bell-like antique cymbals, and below this we hear the snore of horn and bassoons:

Athwart men's noses as they lie asleep

The pace and fascination of the movement are irresistible; it is some of the most ethereally brilliant music ever penned.

Berlioz now draws back from the inner recesses of the imagination and moves towards the tragedy. In his original plan he here reintroduced the choral recitative in a second prologue, unwinding the final stages of the plot. Even though the Garrick sequence was thus made plain, Berlioz was well advised to abandon this scheme and proceed straight to the 'Funeral Procession', itself a feature of eighteenth-century acting versions. The jump is sudden, and we are not given the background to this solemnly moving piece; but that is to judge the sequence by the standards of opera rather than symphony. It is a gravely beautiful movement, utterly characteristic of Berlioz in its use of a long, serpentine fugato, quite pleonastically marked *espressivo*:

EX. 28

The highly charged intervals of this line contrast sharply with the repeated monotone of the Capulets' chorus: 'Jetez des fleurs pour la vierge expirée.' The technique is that of the Offertorium of the *Requiem*, only here the chorus's two notes have been compressed into one, and the fugato made more acrid. The polarity of statuesque solemnity and wailing grief is very striking, and the technical control is extraordinarily skilful. And beautiful though the second half is, turning to the major and reversing the roles of chorus and orchestra, Berlioz cannot quite recapture with voices the expressive density that he drew so tellingly from instruments.

The next section, 'Romeo at the Tomb of the Capulets', is unintelligible without reference to Garrick as Berlioz's note at the head of the score insists. There is also a characteristically poignant remark to the effect that the general public, having no imagination, is unable to make sense of music so reliant on the imagination as this. It is directly descriptive. And this makes it harder, not easier, to appreciate. One has to be entirely submissive to Berlioz's way of doing things to accept the music. If one doubts for a moment the rightness of his thought or the aptness of his description, all is lost. Berlioz certainly approaches nearer the brink of absurdity in this scene than anywhere else in his music, and yet the sheer brain-heat of his imagination, the utter sincerity and fervour of every note, carry the willing listener through to the last drooping phrase, the utter nothingness of the lovers' deaths.

At first the music depicts desperation, as when Dido is first left alone to her despair in the last act of *The Trojans*. 'Tempt not a desperate man,' says Romeo to Paris, laying him low, and forcing access to the tomb. Solemn chords, wide-spaced in pitch and time, suggest the awe of the place, and in a curiously shaped melody scored for cor anglais, four bassoons and one horn in unison, Romeo contemplates Juliet's beauty for the last time, before sinking down under the spell of the poison. 'O true apothecary, thy drugs are quick' were Shakespeare's words, but here Juliet wakes before Romeo is dead. A broken clarinet line recalls the first wind phrases of the 'Love Scene', and the cello line struggles for life. Suddenly the orchestra springs into a frenzied flash-back of the 'Love Scene'. This is the 'delirious joy' of the lovers' final reunion. But the screaming cornets and the restless, hectic harmonies are doomed to annihilation and collapse. The phrases become more fragmentary and deranged – Romeo's final agony – and with two chords Juliet stabs herself. Dido did the same in *The Trojans*:

EX. 29 *a* & *b*

The manly opening of Romeo's oboe melody is transformed into a semitonal slide. Two pizzicato notes on the cellos echo the descent to the depths that marked the death of the first of Berlioz's four great tragic heroines in *The Death of Cleopatra* (1829).

Romantic tastes might have followed Garrick in closing the tragedy there, but Berlioz chooses to finish with the reconciliation of the two families effected by Friar Laurence. The finale is a complex miscellany which employs the same techniques as we find in *Benvenuto Cellini* and *La Nonne sanglante*; it is unashamedly operatic in style. We have been well prepared for this by the vivid action of the previous movement, and the actual voices of Friar Laurence and the chorus bring us down to the level of reality. The finale has been much criticised for its remoteness from some unstated ideal of what a symphonic finale ought to be. But dramatically it is extremely well knit, both within itself and in relation to the rest of the symphony. Its weaknesses are a certain pallor of invention for some of the Friar's narrative; the section 'Mais vous avez repris la guerre de famille' and his appeasing words after the chorus's outburst of family enmity are uncomfortably mechanical and recall Berlioz's earliest style almost to arousing a suspicion that the ideas may have been second-hand in 1839. But the brilliance of the choral writing, Friar Laurence's suave E flat aria, and the grandeur of the closing chorus are sufficient to raise the finale almost to the level of what has gone before.

One is compelled to face the charge that *Romeo and Juliet* is a stylistic miscellany. Berlioz has a single, consistent purpose, but a variety of means of expressing that purpose. The diversity of his approach is as characteristic as Victor Hugo's denial of the classical dramatic unities; there was a positive virtue in throwing together strangely assorted and often deliberately contrasted ingredients as a reflection of the complexity and ruggedness of things. Berlioz's fondness for juxtaposing seemingly incongruous elements in a composite work has already been mentioned. It is not blind unawareness nor ignorance nor poor taste that causes him to do so; it is the deliberate result of his striving to match every subject to its ideal expressive means. The lovers must be expressed orchestrally; Friar Laurence must be expressed vocally. Knowing Berlioz's music for both, we do not complain that the lovers do not sing nor that Friar Laurence could have been better impersonated by instruments. So we should not grumble at the formal diversity of the total work. The term symphony has been stretched to breaking point, but it is the music, not the title, that matters.

SYMPHONIE FUNÈBRE ET TRIOMPHALE

The direction of the symphony in Berlioz's hands is seen in *Romeo and Juliet* to be passing away from the purely instrumental form, and to be plunging deep into the territory of opera and dramatic cantata. Thus the logical course from there is not to the *Funeral and Triumphal Symphony* that followed less than a year later, but to the subsequent major work, *The Damnation of Faust* of 1846. From dramatic symphony to dramatic legend is a natural and straightforward progress; voices and words now cover almost the entire canvas, and Berlioz's unequalled mastery of purely instrumental forces is rarely given later expression. The notable cases of Berlioz reverting to instrumental means for intense dramatic expression are the *Hamlet* march of 1848 and the 'Royal Hunt and Storm' from *The Trojans*.

The apparent discontinuity and lack of formal progress from *Romeo and Juliet* is one of the reasons why the *Funeral and Triumphal Symphony* should be regarded as a throw-back to Berlioz's earlier manner rather than as a successor in the symphonic line. It is a grand ceremonial work commissioned by the Minister of the Interior to celebrate the tenth anniversary of the July Revolution of 1830. It was designed to accompany the solemn reinterment of the remains of the victims of the Three Glorious Days, and was therefore scored for a large military band. Its first movement, the 'Funeral March', was played many times over in the course of the procession, Berlioz in uniform heading the 200 marching musicians; the slow movement, 'Funeral Oration', accompanied the clergy's blessing at the new resting-place, the newly erected column in the Place de la Bastille; and the final movement, 'Apotheosis', was designed to crown the 1830 Revolution in a glorious retrospective triumph. In the event, as Berlioz amusingly recounts in his *Memoirs*, the finale was drowned by the mistimed manoeuvres of the National Guard.

Whatever Berlioz's feelings about revolution (and they were less and less sympathetic as time went on) and whatever the cynicism of the authorities in ordering this commemoration, he treated it as a useful commission and an opportunity to exploit a (for him) new kind of musical sonority. He had nourished grandiose plans for a large-scale, outdoor, patriotic ceremony in 1835, modelled directly on the original revolution-inspired compositions of Gossec and Méhul in the 1790s, and it is likely that some music of the earlier scheme was reshaped for the new symphony. Berlioz said at the time that the composition took him only forty hours; presumably this refers to the drafting of the score, but there are cogent arguments for believing the music to have been written earlier. The second movement can be traced to the unfinished opera *Les Francs Juges*, whose remaining fragments, dating from 1826–8, show the trombone solo in its original form as a tenor recitative and air. Here is the opening strain, marked 'Cavatine':

EX. 30

Tu ne sais pas tra - hir le mal - heur qui t'im - plo re,

Dieu des in - for - tu - nés, tu te plais, ô Som - meil etc.

The fact that the symphony begins in F minor and ends in B flat has occasionally been remarked upon, although no convincing explanation as been offered why Berlioz should have wished to do this in a relatively short work of this kind. We know the central movement was a self-borrowing; at least one other almost certainly was; and the remaining movement was probably a reworking too, otherwise the tonalities would have been brought into line.

We can at least assume that the musical ideas had long been in existence in connection with earlier neo-Napoleonic works contemplated by Berlioz between his Italian journey and the *Requiem* of 1837. The *Requiem* clearly absorbed many of his ideas on the architectural relationship of music and space and on the potential of music in ceremonial. He was to explore this further in the *Te Deum* of 1849. The outdoor purpose of the *Funeral and Triumphal Symphony* was only short-lived, for within two years Berlioz rewrote it, cancelled the original title *Military Symphony*, and added optional parts for strings and, at the end of the 'Apotheosis', for chorus. Berlioz was even later to say that it was unwise to attempt outdoor performances, mainly as a result of his efforts to get a satisfactory result from 1800 performers in the vast open-air Hippodrome in 1846.

The score allows a minimum of 107 participants, but the full forces should include four piccolos, five flutes, five oboes, thirty-three clarinets of different sizes, eight bassoons, twelve horns, eight trumpets, four cornets, eleven trombones, six ophicleides, and eight side-drums. In the last movement there is a part for a 'Turkish crescent', a tall heavily decorated apparatus on which dangled all manner of bells and metal bars. These proportions derive from the normal complement of military bands, and it is as military music within a self-contained tradition rather than as a symphony that the work should be judged. The pervasive sound of high clarinets and the almost hypnotic participation of the side-drums exercise an uncanny fascination. Not until one hears Gossec's incredible *Marche lugubre* of 1790, a full fifty years earlier than Berlioz's symphony, does it seem possible that the sound was not entirely of Berlioz's invention.

Of the three movements the first is undoubtedly the best, although Berlioz himself usually omitted it in performance. It is a solemn and powerful funeral march; the heavy black drapes are barely ever drawn aside. There is a gleam of personal warmth in the second subject, but otherwise the music is stern and granite-like. Once again Berlioz displays his natural gift for long, beautifully wrought melody. The phrases link up one to another in natural succession and build up a powerful twenty-bar span:

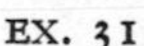

The tempo is very slow. A conductor's skill is severely exercised in judging how slow it can go without stalling, but solemnity and breadth must at all costs form the dominant impression. In place of a development section Berlioz introduces a sinister triplet figure, like giants attempting to dance, punctuated by short, massive chords. But the main theme, with firm downward step from tonic to dominant of the scale appears strongly in the bass before the recapitulation. One of the most striking passages of the movement is the long build-up over a dominant pedal, with the rhythm

generating great coils of energy and arriving at the superb harmonic clash:

EX. 32

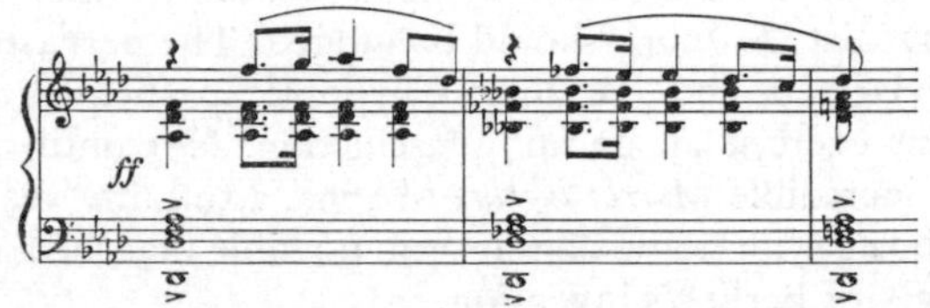

In the reprise this section is heightened by the addition of a long winding counterpoint on bass clarinet, solo trombone, and cellos – an extraordinary timbre.

Weighty chords announce the 'Funeral Oration', declaimed by a solo trombone, first in recitative, then in arioso to a throbbing accompaniment in the horns. Apart from the last eight bars of coda the trombone soloist carves out a long shapely melody and seems to defy attempts by the accompanying wind to break it up into question-and-answer patterns.

The *Apotheosis* breaks across the last G major chord with a stirring roll of drums and an apocalyptic fanfare proclaiming the triumphant B flat tonality. The march itself has a deliberate four-squareness; it risks banality in being populist, in calling on every citizen to wave the tricolour, but comes off by its robust scoring and some harmonic surprises in its middle section. The pace of the movement causes problems because, although a broad tempo is desirable for the opening strain, there are later sections of the movement which press forward. The movement seems to have been conceived at varying speeds; in general the marking *allegro non troppo e pomposo* and the size of the band will support breadth rather than haste.

There is some obvious padding, but the entry of the chorus just before the final strain is extraordinarily effective, and with a stroke of incomparable genius Berlioz shifts his huge armies into a shattering A major a dozen bars from the end; the psychological effect is like the switch to E major at the end of Ravel's *Bolero*. Moreover it emphasises even more triumphantly the brazen B flat tonality of the close.

After the *Funeral and Triumphal Symphony* Berlioz wrote no more symphonies. It would have been difficult to extend the symphonic idea further than in *Romeo and Juliet*, and the stream divides into other channels. However there is in the *Memoirs* an account of a dream in 1852 in which he heard most of a movement of a symphony in A minor. Next day he stopped himself writing it down by the reflection that if he wrote one movement he would have to write the rest. This would take three months and close down other sources of income. If he finished it he would have to have it copied. If he had it copied he would have to have it performed. The certain expense would deprive his ailing wife of daily medical attention and his son of support. He decided to forget it. The next night he heard the symphony again but though he liked it he managed by persistence of will to forget it completely. If it had been written, we may be sure that it would not have been offered to the world as Symphony No. 5 in A minor. Yet the outline of the music of at least one movement was formulated before any suggestion of a descriptive or expressive subject attached itself to the music. This does not imply that poetic images are unimportant and can happily be ignored in Berlioz's music; each one is a direct exposition of his feelings about the music, and thus a crucial and authentic feature of the work itself.

The Marches

Jacques Barzun has drawn attention to the importance of marches in Berlioz's output, and to the variety of types he uses. Features of the march subtly pervade the Viennese classics (Mozart's piano concertos, Schubert's Great C major Symphony), and it was probably from Beethoven's two symphonic marches, the slow movement of the *Eroica* and the tenor solo section of the finale of the Choral Symphony, that Berlioz drew his ideas of an expanded march movement in the context of a symphony. They were also common enough in opera (every Meyerbeer opera has its march) and it was an operatic march, the 'March of the Guards', that became a symphonic march, the 'March to the Scaffold', in the *Fantastic Symphony*. Another pictorial march, the 'Pilgrims' March', followed in *Harold in Italy*. *Romeo and Juliet* has 'Juliet's Funeral Procession', more dirge than march, and the *Funeral and Triumphal Symphony* has, as we have just seen, two full-scale marches, in each of the classic types, a funeral march and a triumphal march. Two marches feature in Berlioz's arrangements of other men's music, the *Marseillaise* arrangement of 1830, with its strikingly Berliozian bass line:

EX. 33

and the brilliant *Moroccan March* of Leopold de Meyer, orchestrated with an added coda in 1845. The piece is dashing, almost comic – and never played.

The best known of Berlioz's marches follows a similar formula, a development and orchestration of a given tune. This is the *Hungarian March*, written for his concert in Budapest in February 1846 when it nearly caused a riot by inflaming patriotic sentiments. Far from being outraged by Berlioz's free treatment of their sacred 'Rakoczy-indulo' the Hungarians responded feverishly, especially to the long build up preceding the final return of the theme. Later in the same year Berlioz incorporated it in *The Damnation of Faust* by naming the locale of the first part of the work as the plains of Hungary. It is a stirring finale to the scene, supplies a rich contrast with the meditative scene that follows, and can easily be justified against the purists who have objected to its remoteness from Goethe's drama. Horns and trumpets stamp out the rhythm of the melody, which is first presented in a delicate wind scoring with piquant string pizzicatos reinforcing salient notes. A full-blooded statement is reserved until after a kind of development where the first phrase of the theme is passed around in the lower registers against the booming of the bass drum, 'simulating the effect of distant cannon'. The cumulative effect is irresistible, and this electric momentum carries right through to the coda, spilling out through C sharp minor to a triumphant close in A major.

The *Funeral March for the Last Scene of Hamlet*, composed in 1848, may reasonably claim to be one of the finest of Berlioz's instrumental works, yet it is strangely neglected. There is barely a movement in the symphonies to match it, and only in certain scenes of *The Trojans* does one have the same overwhelming sense of Berlioz's total mastery of orchestral means for expressive effect. If it were played after an actual performance of *Hamlet* one can barely imagine its capacity to move an audience to the depths. Berlioz published it as the third in a group of three works named (after Ovid) *Tristia*, but never heard it performed. It has a small but significant part for wordless chorus intoning long held unison 'Ahs'. The dry colour of the orchestration, the hypnotic persistence of the Schubertian rhythm

|♩ ♫ ♩ ♩|

and the tragic solemnity of the thematic material create a singular tension, and at the summit of a mighty climax 'a peal of ordnance is shot off'. Double basses tentatively break the hollow silence that ensues, and the music creeps back to life for one of the most heart-rending and pathetic dismissals in musical literature. Soft reverberations rise from the tam-tam, and Berlioz's miraculous falling chromatics entwine:

EX. 34

The last word is given to the chorus holding a unison C long after A minor has faded to nothing.

In less than twenty pages Berlioz has given the effect of culminating an enormous work. The power of the music casts its spell back over the whole play. By itself it is a striking funeral march; in its context it assumes a world of meaning that illuminates both the play and the music. Barely even at the height of *The Trojans*, at Dido's farewell to the city of Carthage, did he equal this epic sense of scale and solemn grandeur; an equivalent awareness of loss and tragedy is sounded in the mime scene of Andromache in the first act of *The Trojans*, but it was only given to Berlioz in his highest maturity to achieve this. The *Hamlet* march ushered in his final mastery, glimpsed in the *Te Deum* of 1849 and bearing fruit in *The Childhood of Christ*, *The Trojans*, and *Beatrice and Benedict*.

The *Te Deum* is a much admired work that has never won universal acclaim. Its heights are undoubtedly Babylonian, as Berlioz himself described them, but I doubt if he would have made extravagant claims for the 'March for the Presentation of the Colours' which is found at the end of the score. Berlioz wished it to be omitted on all but military occasions, and this has been the general practice, especially as it detracts somewhat from the very powerful conclusion that the 'Judex Crederis' setting would otherwise give. Even though it makes thematic reference to the opening chorus, it could well stand as an independent concert piece from time to time. In addition to the large orchestra with quadruple wind for the *Te Deum*, the march calls for a choir of twelve harps which join in the last refrain with thunderous angelic voice. The refrain itself is in a bracing dotted rhythm in eight-bar sequences, and it looks forward to the 'Trojan March' by its arrival on a chord of A flat half way through. It looks back to the 'Apotheosis' march (all three are in B flat) in the first episode, where persistent triplets effectively transform the time signature into 12/8. The second episode reviews the fugal material of the opening chorus, and elaborates the bold but rather mysterious descending scale presented by the organ in the twelfth bar of the work. A third episode, with brilliant parts for the cornets and a high saxhorn, was later cut by Berlioz. After the *Hungarian March* and the 'Apotheosis' it is difficult not to register disappointment that Berlioz has no trick of tonality up his sleeve for the final peroration. He does introduce the descending scale on the organ in combat with the march in the entire orchestra, but otherwise its effect rests on brute force.

Not all Berlioz's marches spring from the grandiose and ceremonial side of his musical nature. The 'Pilgrims' March' is of a quite different order, and it is this more restrained manner that recurs in two character marches in the last works, the 'Nocturnal March' in *The Childhood of Christ* and the 'Wedding March' in *Beatrice and Benedict*. The latter is strictly outside our purview; it is a choral hymn with traces of martial rhythm and a contrasting counter-theme. Nor is the 'Nocturnal March' to be regarded as a concert piece. It is inseparable from the dramatic and imaginative scheme of 'Herod's Dream', the first part of the trilogy, and it wonderfully suggests the darkened streets patrolled by Roman soldiers.

The grand marches are more hymns to *la gloire* than music to march to, and the 'Trojan March' is very much a national hymn, more a symbol of the Trojan people than an occasional march. It runs through the whole of *The Trojans*, following the triumphs and tribulations of Priam's people. After the performances of the second half of the opera in the autumn of 1863 Berlioz wrote a concert arrangement of the march with a view to having it performed by the private concert societies that were springing up under Pasdeloup, Colonne and others. The arrangement was never in fact played in his lifetime.

It starts as a compressed version of the finale of Act I and then joins on to the closing bars of the first tableau of Act V. Berlioz has added a number of small details to link up the different extracts. As in the *Hungarian March* the rhythm of the refrain is hammered out on one note by the brass before the melody itself is presented. Although it begins on the simple notes of an arpeggio the theme is extraordinarily rousing. With superb sangfroid it plunges straight into A flat after four bars, and finds its way back by a shifting alternation of two harmonies:

EX. 35

A new theme appears in G minor, much weaker than the first, and though both rely extensively on triplet groupings, what was strength in the first theme is frailty in the second. By transferring itself to F major it gains weight and also prepares for the return to B flat. The climax grows, created in the opera by the approach from the distance of the cortège bringing the Wooden Horse within the city walls; a string tremolo rises out of the depths and a *fortissimo* crash halts the music. A clash of armour has sounded from within the horse and the Trojans pause momentarily on the brink of sanity before deciding to hurl themselves more vigorously at their doomed task. An exciting version of the alternating chords under the rhythmic fanfare

Ex. 36

foreshadows the future destiny of the Trojan people, and the march rings out triumphantly and optimistically in B flat major.